Old RAMSEY

by
Steven Dearden & Ken Hassell

In the early nineteenth century increasing use of Ramsey's harbour made it necessary to provide a new quay and more shelter at the harbour approach. Developments began in the 1820s and by 1845, with a new North Pier under construction, about 45 yards of the South Pier were raised and a stone lighthouse constructed as shown in this exceptionally early photograph by George Patterson. Work on replacing this structure was completed by 1876 and little survives from the era before a promenade or proper sea wall. However, The Prince of Wales Hotel to the left of the lighthouse has much changed. Originally Marine Mansion, it had become the Marine Inn by 1871 and was later the Neptune Hotel before being extended and completely refurbished by the Prince of Wales Company in 1884.

In the 1860s Thomas Gibson & Co. ran a shipbuilding industry in Ramsey shipyard, employing between three hundred and four hundred men. The company quickly went bankrupt and the yard passed through several hands, getting smaller and smaller. However, Ramsey shipbuilders produced some illustrious vessels. The first ever oil tanker, the *Jane*, was launched here in 1863, while probably the most famous vessel built in the yard was the three-masted *Euterpe*, which, renamed *Star of India*, is now a floating museum in San Diego, California. The last of the half-decker 'cod boats', the *Master Frank*, built by Messrs Clucas and Duggan in 1894, can still be seen in Ramsey harbour, beautifully restored. By 1895 the shipyard was in decline and this photograph shows conversion work being carried out for the salt works which commenced production in 1903.

© Ken Hassell & Steven Dearden, 2000
First published in the United Kingdom, 2000,
by Stenlake Publishing, Ochiltree Sawmill, The Lade,
Ochiltree, Ayrshire, KA18 2NX
Telephone / Fax: 01290 423114

ISBN 1 84033 094 5

INTRODUCTION

Although Ballure Chapel is the only building built before 1800 that survives, Ramsey is an ancient settlement. The gently sloping beaches were ideal for Viking longships; Godred Crovan landed in 1079 and Olave was assassinated by his nephew, Reginald, near the harbour in 1154. Robert Bruce landed in 1313 on his way to Castle Rushen and in 1651 Colonel Duckingfield also used Ramsey to land and take possession of the Island for the Parliamentary forces.

None of these brief, historical references make mention of a town or village, however. In 1630 the sea carried away a large portion of the settlement and by 1726 the population was only 460. It was not until John Feltham's *Tour Through the Island of Mann in 1797 and 1798*, the first travel book to describe Ramsey in any detail, that Ramsey is spoken of as 'a small neat town containing about three hundred houses'. As it was then, the town stood on an island between the Sulby River and the sea. One branch of the river flowed into the hills of the Mooragh Brooghs and was defended by a fort. The other, filled in 1835, flowed into a lake on the site of the Market Place and entered the bay a little south of the Old Cross, at the top of Church Street.

Ramsey was the capital of the north, the market town and only port of an extensive fishing and agricultural district. Its admirable situation in the centre of the largest and best sheltered bay in the Island, and backed by richly wooded hills, also gave it special advantages as a holiday resort. By the 1850s the fashion for an annual seaside holiday was spreading down through the ranks of shopkeepers and white-collar workers, reaching the skilled operatives. Before long it became almost universal amongst workers in the Lancashire textile districts. Helped by cheap rail travel to the coast, the working class seaside holiday became a phenomenon of the last quarter of the nineteenth century and the Manx resorts had to be made economically accessible to benefit.

Prior to the opening of the first railway in 1873, most visitors came to Douglas as travel to other locations by land was difficult and mainly by horseback. In order to land at Ramsey, small boats had to be employed and passengers carried ashore at a small wooden landing place just north of where the Queen's Pier was later built. Ramsey was finally connected to the railway system in 1879 and the low water landing pier followed in 1887, ensuring that the town did not miss out on tourist development.

Douglas was noted for it's gregarious approach to holidaymaking; informality was the order of the day and families holidaying with children were rare. Ramsey aimed to appeal more to families in search of a restful holiday, the new breed of middle class visitor 'pursuing gentility on two

or three pounds per week'.

The key to success lay in the variety of social, cultural and recreational facilities that could be offered. The provision of accommodation for holidaymakers became the single most important economic activity, bringing with it all the problems of relying on the vagaries of a short holiday season. The health and comfort of visitors was essential and municipal spending and intervention grew in importance accordingly. In 1865 Ramsey was incorporated as a town with seven town commissioners but it was the building boom of the 1880s that saw the real growth.

Practically all the major holiday resorts in Britain had been established by the 1870s and Douglas was by that time the only major resort on the Island. Extending an established town was less uncertain than the creation of a resort out of nothing, but nevertheless Ramsey still underwent massive changes in the period 1880 to 1900. It is a testament to the success of the developers that the town grew to have such a pleasing variety of amenities and handsome buildings on fine, regularly laid out streets. The town was little altered again until the redevelopments of the 1960s. Unfortunately, these meant that the old Ramsey of the eighteenth century smuggling period, with it's narrow winding streets and lanes and old fashioned houses, was largely lost. However, it continues to be a prosperous residential town and much that is admirable remains.

A Lifeboat Day launching of the lifeboat *Mary Isabella II*. Between 1896 and 1915 the vessel was called out forty-eight times and saved 153 lives.

This view of the harbour from the 1880s predates the construction of the swing bridge which played a vital part in the development of the Mooragh. The project was launched in August 1887 but following financial problems and difficulties in getting a firm foundation for the centre platform, the official opening was delayed until 1892. The Trafalgar Inn and the Stanley Inn can be seen on the quay, although some of the other buildings have been redeveloped over the last 120 years.

RAMSAY HARBOUR, ISLE OF MAN. 3548 J.V.

Some particularly fine cod are on offer at this pre-1914 fish auction in front of the Union Hotel. The cod were caught on heavy lines hundreds of feet in length. A hook was attached to the line every few feet and baited with whelk, or 'buckie' as they were locally known. Preparations would be done in the harbour and each finished line would become a neat coil about two feet in diameter, ready for the evening sailing.

In the 1930s the Ramsey Steamship Company lost three vessels: the *Ben Blanche*, the *Ben Vooar I* and the *Ben Seyr* which was tragically lost with all hands on 2 October 1938. The *Cargan*, a 274 ton coaster, was bought in 1938 and was renamed the *Ben Vooar II*. Eventually sold for scrap in 1956, she is the ship nearest to the quay wall in this photograph. The other ship is the *S.S. Manxona*, built in 1921 for the Manx Salt and Alkali Company which was based in Ramsey. A familiar sight in the harbour over many years, she arrived on her maiden voyage under Captain Robert Cleator in March 1922. Under Captain Robert Kelly, later with his son J.E.P. Kelly as mate, she carried all manner of general cargoes as well as the thousands of tons of salt processed by the Ramsey salt works. She left Ramsey for the last time in December 1948 on her way to many more years service in Scandinavian waters.

The quayside was, as now, a busy place with coal, timber, manufactured goods and other commodities being landed. Metal ores, blocks of salt and animal foodstuffs were the main exports. Indeed, when the *Ben Seyr* was lost on her way to the Bristol Channel in October 1938, she was carrying a cargo of oats. By the time of this photograph, taken sometime before 1914, the railway track had been laid part of the way along the East Quay to facilitate loading but the horse and cart were still the usual means of moving agricultural produce.

Prior to the Bridges Act of 1739 the old roads generally crossed rivers by means of fords and even local goods for other locations on the Island were transported by sea. There were fords near the present town hall and at Greenland but neither were passable at high water. The first request for a bridge by the inhabitants of Ramsey seems only to have been made in 1728. The act provided for five bridges including the one 'over that river between Ramsey and Kirk Bride and Kirk Andreas' that can be seen in this photograph from around 1905. The 180 foot stone bridge, sometimes called the 'gateway to the north', became particularly important after the opening of the Ramsey shipyard in the 1850s. The bridge was widened in 1840 and improved to much its present form in 1888 when a bill was passed through the Keys releasing the Ramsey ratepayers from the burden of maintaining it.

The *Hindenburg* flying over the salt works chimney on 26 June 1936. She was returning from New York, flying in a south-easterly direction at a height of 1,000 feet and travelling at between 80 and 90 m.p.h. Apparently, one of the passengers on this trip was world champion boxer Max Schmelling, returning from his victory over Joe Louis. Swastikas were clearly visible on her tail fins and, at a time of increasing tension with Germany, questions about this in the House of Commons led to flights over British coastal waters being stopped. The following year the *Hindenburg* burst into flames on her arrival in New Jersey and was destroyed in only two minutes.

Built at Peel around 1912, the *Ben Varrey* became a well-known local boat.
Captained by Philip Kneale of the Lhen, she was a fishing boat throughout
the years of the First World War but by the 1920s was frequently chartered
by parties of visitors, as seen here. Deemster Cowley and Jim Bell were
among the locals who sometimes went on pleasure trips in her to the west
of Scotland. In later years she was owned by Harry Quayle, a Harbour
Board worker who was often to be seen in charge of the swing bridge.
The *Ben Varrey* was eventually sold to a new owner in Shoreham, Kent.

This vessel is the smack *Excelsior*, skippered by Captain Leadbeater, who,
according to the message on the back, was eighty-nine at the time of this
photograph. Behind, the North Pier still looks much the same as it did
when originally constructed in 1864 (although the wooden structure had
since been cased in concrete to resist winter storms).

This 1931 photograph shows the Customs House berth of the harbour, the area known as the 'Commercial Corner'. Well-known local fisherman John Crix was for many years skipper-owner of the half decker Penguin, along with his brother William. On the left is the stern of the Castletown registered Steam Packet coaster *Tyrconnel*, a familiar sight in Ramsey.

A surprisingly high proportion of the town's trading was once done from the Market Place, including the familiar fish sales and weekly furniture sales run by Chrystal's. Carts would bring in farm produce from the countryside and the stalls on the Dale Street side offered everything from chickens at 1/6d and rabbits at 1/-, to toffee and gingerbread men. The butcher stalls were lined up in front of St Paul's Church and perhaps as many as eighty lambs were killed, ready for the Saturday market. On Saturday nights a raised platform, illuminated by paraffin lamps, housed a salesman selling stomach powders and a black man who extracted teeth using just his thumb and index finger!

A procession through the Market Place by the 1st Ramsey Scout Troop. The pioneer Scout in Ramsey was Norman Cannell. He started as a self-appointed patrol leader in 1909 and by November that year had organised three patrols, the Curlews, the Peewits and the Lions. He persuaded an uncle, Mr J. Marshall to take charge as Scoutmaster and by March 1910 there were thirty-three members. The Mona Tea Rooms on Market Place may be better remembered as Limna's Manx Kipper Stores.

On signs within the image:

MN 9295

..L 94
..SONS
..RLIAMENT ST.
..R COACH
..RIETORS.
10 .. DAILY
FRO..
MARKET
SQUARE
2.30 ..
Sunday
Afternoon
.. ..
SWIMMING POOL
..RADOYL BAY

BOOK HERE
FOR
AFTERNOON DRIVE
ROUND-THE NORTH
-AND-
POINT-OF-AYRE
-VIA-
BRIDE-LHEN-JURBY
BALLAUGH-SULBY-
LEAVING 2-30
RETURN 5-30

BOOK HERE
FOR
NIARBYL BAY
VIA
SULBY-BALLAUGH-
MICHAEL-PEEL-
RETURN
VIA
St.JOHNS AND
GLEN HELEN.
LEAVE 2-30..
RETURN 6-0..
FARES 9/d

CRENNELL'S PRIVATE

Crennells De-Luxe Coaches

This photograph of the Market Square shows the friendly rivalry between the coach firms looking for holiday business. It was taken in 1937, in the days when holidaymakers stayed 'full board' and spent their time taking afternoon coach trips. The coach on the left belongs to John Dawson of Auckland Terrace, Parliament Street, who was also the owner of the Station Garage on Bowring Road. Crennell's, on the right, will be a name still familiar to locals, although more now for their taxi service.

14

Mooragh Park & Lake, Ramsey I. o. M.

By 1900 the bridge and channel to the bottom left of this early view of Mooragh Park had disappeared. Not much evidence is visible of the 30,000 trees that had been planted but it is still difficult to believe that only dunes and the old river bed had occupied the site five years before this photograph was taken. Prior to the redevelopment the chief sport in Ramsey had been archery and the butts were situated in the sand dunes. The island in the lake was intended to contain a fountain and tennis courts but access to them and the number of balls lost by players quickly put an end to this attraction!

MOORAGH PARK, RAMSEY.

The park, 1935. At the south end of the lake a landing stage and a café with a veranda were constructed. Teas and yacht hire were available there, as they are today, although deck chairs are now an unusual sight. Ballacloan, the National Children's Home, can be seen across the lake on Windsor Mount.

Troops on the Mooragh, 1904. The open ground here was used for volunteer encampments from 1892 up to 1914. Rather alarmingly, the troop's heavy guns, aimed at the beach, would be drawn up between the road and the footpath for artillery practice; in 1892 there had been controversy when the South Lancashire Artillery Volunteers had been prohibited from Sunday afternoon practice by the High Bailiff. The path was once the track bed of the Mooragh railway, a little known temporary line laid in 1888 for the extensive development work in progress at the time.

BATHING POOL CAFÉ & S.S. PEEL CASTLE, RAMSEY. I.O.M.

E.2223.

The newly constructed Pool Ballroom, 1935. John Hughes of Ramsey Amusements had taken over the swimming pool in 1933 and successfully extended the facilities to include a beginners pool and a ballroom. By this period the *Peel Castle* (on the right) was often limited to cargo duties and excursion trips, but she still maintained the direct Friday sailing from Liverpool to Ramsey. In 1926 it had been hoped to use her to initiate a passenger service to Workington and an excursion in September of that year saw 1,300 northern residents embark on her for a day trip to Cumberland. The regular service never materialised, although for many years Workington Town Band promoted their own bank holiday excursion to Ramsey.

The Ramsey Palace was erected on the site of Elm Villa in 1892 but the controlling company quickly ran into financial difficulties. However, it stayed open and extensive alterations were made in 1912 by Manx Picturedromes Limited, owners of the Grand Theatre in Douglas. The Palace was never a great financial success and passed through several owners until its conversion into the Plaza in 1935. It was demolished in 1991. Pictured here from Peel Street, the Palace already housed the Manx Electric Railway staff quarters and had diversified its attractions to include a roller skating rink, a great craze of the Edwardian period.

Peel Street, 1937, looking away from the Plaza. Pegram's Stores on the left also had branches in Douglas and Peel and advertised that orders were delivered daily by motor services in town and surrounding districts.

A military band playing in the Court House gardens in the 1920s. Rebuilt in its present style in 1840, the Mitre Hotel next to D. Vondy's was first mentioned in Feltham's *Tour* when it was called the King's Head and kept by Cornelius Hinds. In 1814 it was renamed by the new owner Charles Richardson, former licensee of the Crown and Mitre in Kirk Michael.

Stead and Simpson's shoe shop in Parliament Street, 1906.

Parliament Street, 1937. Next door to T. Kneale's boot and shoe repairers is the Plough Hotel, a favourite of the farmers on market day. It has been known by that name since at least 1824 and was built by a Jurby mason, John Kelly, in 1806.

Parliament Street, Ramsey, Isle of Man.

Looking the other way down Parliament Street. Auckland Terrace to the left remains the same but the buildings on the right from Ramsey Motors to the Trinity Primitive Methodist chapel were demolished in 1958. The chapel was completed in 1892 by Mr W.C. Southward of Sulby and led to a division in the congregation with the older Independent Methodist chapel in Chapel Lane. The rival groups were later reunited and the location will now be familiar as the site of A.J. Millichap's furniture store.

In the summer of 1919 visitors returned to the Island in nearly their pre-war numbers and the Manx economy regained confidence after the problems of the war years. This mood of confidence was helped by the two day visit of King George V with Queen Mary and Princess Mary in July 1920. They arrived at Ramsey pier before touring the Island and are seen here outside the old town hall on Parliament Square.

The visit of George VI and Queen Elizabeth in July 1945 was the first journey the royal couple had made together outside the United Kingdom since the beginning of the war. It came about because Lady Margaret Rose, wife of Earl Granville, was the elder sister of Queen Elizabeth and the visit marked a successful conclusion to his period as Lieutenant Governor. King George is standing with Earl Granville talking to members of the Home Guard outside Jack Pyatt's shop on Parliament Square.

An Empire Day gathering at Albert Road School just prior to 1914. The figures on the dais include the Rev. Mark Harrison and Mr E.T. Shepherd, headmaster from 1905 to 1917. The boys in the background were presumably not pupils at the school as the headmaster was fond of announcing from the top of the stairs at the back of the school: 'Scholars, there is a lovely flat-topped wall around the playground, but the first scholar who walks on that wall will not walk home!'

This decorated float with a Red Cross theme was the entry in Ramsey's 1911 George V Coronation celebrations from Cronk Bane Farm in Bride. A Mark McJoughin was the owner of Cronk Bane quarterland before 1600 and the land has remained in the ownership of the Joughin family ever since.

In 1930 the Ramsey Ladies' Cushag Choir won the prestigious Lester Jones Trophy and Downey Shield at the London Music Festival. On their return to the Island, they were also awarded the Manx Society Rose Bowl at the 'Guild' (the popular name for the Manx Music Festival which is still held every year). The triumphant choir members were:
Back row: (left to right) Mrs Wright, Mrs Fallowfield, Annie Coffey, Gloria Glover, Marjorie Woodward, Ethel Cain, Connie Edmondson, Fanny Tennant, Lily Taylor.
Middle row: Nessie Cleator, Dorothy Crowe, Mrs Kelly, Maude Callister, Edith Stephenson, Mrs Byrne, Eva Kneale, Minna Graves, Betty L. Callister, Josie Graves, Marie Gelling.
Front row: Mona Quayle, Chrissie Lace, Mrs Troughton, Mrs Poland, Mary Purcell Black (conductress), the accompanist from London, Mona Kee, Mrs E. Kewin, Kitty Purcell, Marjorie Kissack, Mona Corlett, Dora Wright, Edith Brew, Peggy Joughin.

A carnival parade passing down Waterloo Road by the junction with Victoria Road, *c.* 1930. Sadly, all the property behind Waterloo Road to the right was demolished in the 1960s and the much missed second branch of the Co-op can also be seen in the distance at the junction with Approach Road. Their Waverley House premises had earlier been an eating house owned by the Coule family. Their premises were more central than might be thought as the horse drawn wagonettes carrying holidaymakers would enter Ramsey down Waterloo Road to this point before turning right to the Old Cross and along Church Street to the Market Place.

Waterloo Road, 1937: a reminder of the days when buses connecting with the ferry services could be sure of collecting holidaymakers and their cases at every stop in the town. Fortunately, people rarely had much luggage in pre-war days, leisure wear for men at least still being a vague concept. This twenty-eight seat Leyland Lion PLSC1 entered service with Manxland Bus Services in 1927 and was transferred to Isle of Man Railway Co. Ltd and then subsequently to Isle of Man Road Services Ltd. It wasn't withdrawn until 1950.

Following the success of the 1904 and 1905 Gordon Bennett Trials, the first Tourist Trophy race took place in September 1905. The course followed the Trials route, heading towards Jurby from Ballaugh and approaching Ramsey via Sandygate. W. Parker Thomas is seen here in his Argyll car approaching the remarkably unchanged corner of Jurby Road with Bowring Road. Parker Thomas was destined to finish in only eighth place over an hour behind the winner, John Napier.

The most northerly siding of Ramsey Station continued through the station (which was otherwise a terminus) and across Bowring Road to form the Ramsey Quay line. It could take up to two days to unload a cargo at Ramsey. A few empty wagons would be pushed to the ship-side and, once loaded, pushed into one of the sidings until a rake of wagons was ready to be taken away by an engine. The East Quay track was removed in 1925 and the West Quay in 1956, having last been used in 1952. This rare photograph of the line shows engine no.3 'Pender' of 1873, last used in 1959 and now an exhibit in the Manchester Museum of Science and Industry.

The Beyer Peacock engine no.11 'Maitland' of 1905, pictured outside Ramsey Station preparing for the return trip to Douglas. 'Maitland' has rarely been out of service, spending most of her career with the old Isle of Man Railway based at Douglas on the Ramsey and Peel lines, and today she still runs regular services on the Port Erin line. This photograph dates from 1953, the year of the Island's lowest number of visitors since 1933, war years excepted. Traffic on the Ramsey line also suffered from the partial closure of RAF Jurby, the biggest source of income for the route.

A Douglas bound train climbs gently towards Lezayre, passing Edwardian boaters on the Sulby River. Even in high season a Ramsey train would rarely exceed two carriages and a break van in length. The busiest train was often the last of the day, the 9.30, arriving at Sulby Bridge around 9.45, just in time for a last drink at the Ginger Hall Hotel. In the days before buses and common car ownership it was a long walk for many to St Judes, Sandygate or Ballaugh Cronk.

West of the bridge over the Auldyn, the railway crossed the Sulby by an 80 foot wrought iron girder bridge, nicknamed the 'basket bridge' due to the stretcher which connected its bowstrings. The structure formerly belonged to the Manx Northern Railway and it gave particular concern to the Isle of Man Railway Company after they took over the line; they finally replaced it in November 1914. In dreadful weather the new spans were mounted alongside the old and the old bridge slid bodily northwards on to wooden beams. A train was able to test the new structure that same afternoon – an impressively rapid piece of work.

COTTAGE HOSPITAL. RAMSEY. I.O.M.

Opened in 1908, the Cottage Hospital soon expanded from its original ten beds but continued to be maintained by voluntary contributions until 1948. Donations and legacies contributed to its growth, as well as money raising days known as 'Hospital Saturdays' or 'Sundays'. The first ambulance was purchased in 1912 and from April 1909 Annie Proctor commenced her record thirty-eight years in charge as Matron.

Glen Auldyn post office and stores was only in business between 1930 and 1944 and photographs of the diminutive building are rare. The first postmistress was Emily J. Farager and in 1933 she was replaced by Elsie Tyson, who continued in charge until closure. Business could never have been great at a time before much of the present day property in Glen Auldyn was built. Without the summer trade from campers and walkers, it is surprising that it stayed open so far into the war.

The Fern Glen resort at the top of Glen Auldyn was a successful attraction in the inter-war years, patronised by walkers and passengers of the special bus service. A steep climb from the gardens led right up through the glen to the mountain road. The putting green and playground offered a cooler alternative on a hot afternoon.

An interior view of the café at Fern Glen from 1937 shows two visitors enjoying the speciality strawberry and cream teas. The café and attractions were run by Mrs Lindsay whose husband, Jimmy, ran the tobacconists on the corner of East Street and Parliament Street. This first opened in 1893 and was in business longer than any other tobacconist on the Island.

The height of Edwardian seaside fashion is on display in this view of the lifeboat slipway. Blazers and boater hats continued to be popular for the men for many years and sailor suits remained popular for children, although girls were equally likely to be wearing frilled white dresses with elaborate sun-bonnets. Everyone wore hats, largely to avoid the stigma of a tan, and the ladies' were usually of straw with a dark ribbon and perhaps a veil.

Fred Buxton was a remarkable showman of the old school, a fine tenor vocalist and a gifted composer of popular ballads. As he became established in Douglas, a Ramsey pierrot troupe led by his son soon started to operate successfully from a stage by the Prince of Wales Hotel. A proper covered stage was added to the existing platform in 1899. The takings came from the sale of sheet music, 'lucky' programmes and 'bottling' which involved shaking collection bags coaxingly around the crowd. On a good day there might be such a weight of coppers that the violinist had to carry them away in his instrument case.

ARRIVAL KING'S OWN ROYAL LANCS REG. RAMSEY, I.O.M. 1908.

The Midland Railway Company's *T.S.S. Donegal* arrives at the Queen's Pier in August 1908 with soldiers from the King's Own Royal Lancashire Regiment arriving for their annual camp at Milntown. The Donegal was one of three vessels built for the inauguration of the Belfast – Heysham service in 1904 and unfortunately the only one to be lost during the First World War. Two months after this photograph was taken she went aground west of the Point of Ayre but was refloated the next day with the help of her sister ship the *T.S.S. Antrim*.

The original toll houses, constructed by local builder Edward Gawne, at the entrance to the Queen's Pier, 1928. The pier was still lit by gas at this time. The current entrance was built in front of the toll houses in the winter of 1955-56. It is to be hoped that the money will soon be found to restore this priceless asset to the town.

Tramcar 21 at Ramsey Station, prior to 1914. Dating from 1899, winter saloon 21 has been a mainstay of summer and winter traffic ever since, except between 1990 and 1992 following a disastrous fire at the Derby Castle depot. When the first tram came into Ramsey the directors found they had no station staff to greet it and they 'borrowed' the steam railway station master Malcolm Quayle to stand in for the reception. The centenary of the M.E.R. reaching the Ramsey terminus was celebrated one hundred years to the day on 24 July 1999.

On the night of 26 June 1927, the Fleetwood steam trawler *Cevic* was wrecked on the beach at Granch, south of Ballure. Six men were bravely rescued by the Ramsey lifeboat *Matthew Simpson* under coxswain John Garrett on her first service call. Difficulties arose for the *Cevic* when an easterly gale unexpectedly sprang up while the captain and three of the crew were ashore and unable to return. It was the third time that the ship's fifteen year old apprentice had been wrecked in his short career. The remains of the wreck can still be seen today.

Claughbane Walk, Ramsey, I.O.M.

Starting from the White Gate at the top of May Hill, the walk 'round Claughbane' has always been a favourite for visitors and locals alike. After passing the old mansion and farm buildings, walkers reached the orchard and footpath to Glen Auldyn, the disused quarry, and eventually emerged on to the new mountain road by Elfin Glen and the Hairpin bend. It remains a fine evening walk despite the unfortunate damage caused by property developers.

LEWAIGUE CAMP. RAMSEY. I.O.M.

The Territorial camps in the Ramsey area are particularly associated with Milntown but there were also extensive camps at Lezayre as this 1920s postcard shows. The photograph was taken from the Dreemskerry road, looking across the Manx Electric Railway lines to Ballaterson West.